Space Quest:

Jump to Jupiter

By Peter Lock

Series Editor Deborah Lock
US Senior Editor Shannon Beatty
Editor Arpita Nath
Project Art Editor Hoa Luc
Art Editor Rashika Kachroo
DTP Designers Ashok Kumar and Anita Yadav
Picture Researcher Surya Sankash Sarangi
Producer, Pre-production Ben Marcus
Managing Editor Soma B. Chowdhury
Managing Art Editor Ahlawat Gunjan
Art Director Martin Wilson

Reading Consultant
Linda Gambrell, Ph.D.

First American Edition, 2015
Published in the United States by DK Publishing
345 Hudson Street, New York, New York 10014

The publisher would like to thank the following for their kind permission to reproduce their photographs:
(Key: a-above; b-below/bottom; c-center; f-far; l-left; r-right; t-top)
1 NASA: ESA and E. Karkoschka (U. Arizona) (t). 4 NASA: JPL-Caltech (b). 5 Dreamstime.com: Julien Tromeur (br). 6-7 Alamy Images: Paul Fleet (t). 7 Dreamstime.com: Julien Tromeur (br). 8-9 Corbis: Denis Scott. 11 Dreamstime.com: Alexokokok (c/Frame). 12 Getty Images: Juan Gartner. 12-13 NASA: JPL-Caltech / SETI Institute. 13 Alamy Images: Gl0ck (c). Getty Images: Juan Gartner (cla). NASA: HiRISE / MRO / LPL (U. Arizona) (cra). NASA: (t). 14 Corbis: (crb). 14-15 NASA: JPL-Caltech / SETI Institute. 15 NASA: ESA and E. Karkoschka (U. Arizona) (tr). 16 Corbis: Ron Miller / Stocktrek Images (t). 17 Dreamstime.com: Julien Tromeur (br). 18-19 Corbis: Denis Scott (t). 18 Alamy Images: RGB Ventures / SuperStock. 19 NASA: ESA and E. Karkoschka (U. Arizona) (tr). 20-21 NASA and The Hubble Heritage Team (AURA/STScI). 21 Dreamstime.com: Julien Tromeur (br). 24-25 NASA: (c); JPL-Caltech / SETI Institute. 26-27 NASA: JPL-Caltech / SETI Institute. 28 Alamy Images: Tristan3D (tl). 30 Corbis: NASA - JPL / Science Faction (ca). Dreamstime.com: Alexokokok (t/Frame). 31 Dreamstime.com: Julien Tromeur (br). 32-33 Corbis: NASA - JPL / Science Faction. 34-35 Alamy Images: Trevor Smithers ARPS. 35 Dreamstime.com: Julien Tromeur (br). 36 Alamy Images: NASA / World History Archive & ARPL (tl). Corbis: Denis Scott (t/Background). 37 Dreamstime.com: Julien Tromeur (br). 38-39 Alamy Images: Zoonar GmbH (t). 40-41 NASA: (Jupiter's moons); JPL-Caltech / SETI Institute. 40 Alamy Images: Science Photo Library (b). Corbis: NASA-JPL-Caltech - digital versi / Science Faction (crb). 41 Alamy Images: NASA / World History Archive & ARPL (tc). Corbis: (ca); NASA-JPL-Caltech - digital versi / Science Faction (cla); NASA / Roger Ressmeyer (cb). NASA: JPL / University of Arizona / University of Colorado (bc). 42 123RF.com: Urs Flueeler (clb). Corbis: Logan Mock-Bunting (cla). Dreamstime.com: Eric Isselee (br)
Jacket images: *Front:* Dreamstime.com: Surachet Khamsuk / Surachetkhamsuk tr.
Back: Dorling Kindersley: NASA tl. Dreamstime.com: Clearviewstock (background).
All other images © Dorling Kindersley
For further information see: www.dkimages.com

A WORLD OF IDEAS:
SEE ALL THERE IS TO KNOW

www.dk.com

Contents

4 **Asteroid Belt**

12 Asteroids Up Close

14 Jupiter Data File

16 **Jupiter**

24 Jupiter's Weather

26 *Galileo* Mission

28 **Jupiter's Moons**

40 Moon Zoom

42 Gas Facts

43 Jupiter Quiz

44 Glossary

45 Index

46 Guide for Parents

Asteroid Belt

The asteroid belt is a large ring of rocks between the planets Mars and Jupiter. These rocks of all shapes and sizes are called asteroids. Asteroids are the leftover rocks from when the planets of our solar system were forming millions of years ago.

Many asteroids look like giant potatoes. They are covered in craters and troughs where they crashed into each other.

Some of these rocks are whizzing around at three miles (five km) per second. They go at different speeds and some move in wobbly twists because of their strange, uneven shapes.

The **solar system** includes the Sun and everything that goes around it, such as the planets and asteroids.

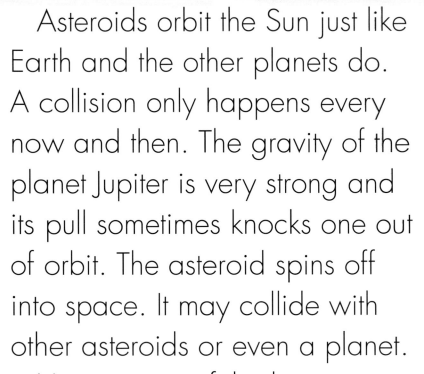

Asteroids orbit the Sun just like Earth and the other planets do. A collision only happens every now and then. The gravity of the planet Jupiter is very strong and its pull sometimes knocks one out of orbit. The asteroid spins off into space. It may collide with other asteroids or even a planet.

Vesta is one of the larger asteroids. It has a giant crater that was made when another asteroid crashed into it. The smash made many small rocks, which scattered into space. Some of these have fallen to Earth as meteorites.

Scientists calculate there are about 1.4 million rocks in the **asteroid belt**.

The largest object in the asteroid belt is Ceres. Ceres looks different than other asteroids because it is round and white. It is known as an icy dwarf planet. It may have an ocean under its icy surface and have more fresh water on it than on Earth.

Space probes (robotic spacecrafts) have been sent on missions to the asteroid belt to look closer at asteroids. In 2011, the *Dawn* probe arrived at Vesta. It then arrived at Ceres in March 2015. The probe sends pictures back to a laboratory on Earth as it orbits the asteroid.

The asteroid belt divides the four planets closest to the Sun (Mercury, Venus, Earth, and Mars) from the four large outer planets (Jupiter, Saturn, Uranus, and Neptune). The inner planets are solid and rocky. The outer planets are mostly made up of gases around a small core of rock or ice at their center.

On the farthest side of the asteroid belt is Jupiter. This is the king of the planets! It has two and a half times the mass of all the other planets together. Almost 1,300 Earths would fit inside this giant world.

Colorful clouds of gases swirl around, making Jupiter bulge out and in. Its surface is always on the move.

Asteroids Up Close

Are these the pieces that tried to form planets billions of years ago?

Uneven surface

Crater

Look at the evidence:

- uneven shapes with craters where collisions have happened
- some are balls of rubble where fragments have clumped together
- they follow orbital paths around the Sun
- some even have small moons of their own orbiting them

Are all asteroids gray?

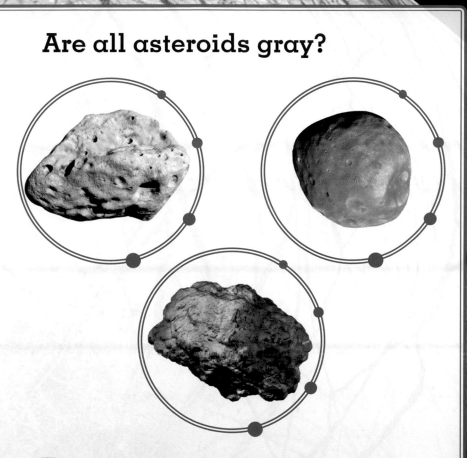

The most common asteroids are gray.
They are rocky, and are found on
the outer edge of the asteroid belt.
Other asteroids can be greenish
to reddish in color. These contain
some metals, and are found on the
inner part of the belt. The asteroids
made of metals are red, and are found
in the middle areas of the belt.

Jupiter Data File

Location: fifth planet from the Sun

Landscape: thick layers of swirling gas clouds with a small core

Size: 11 times larger than Earth

Length of day: 9 Earth hours and 55 minutes

Length of year: 12 Earth years

Pulling power

The gravity of Jupiter is two and a half times stronger than Earth's gravity. This means that its pulling power affects space objects. More than 60 moons orbit Jupiter, caught by its gravity.

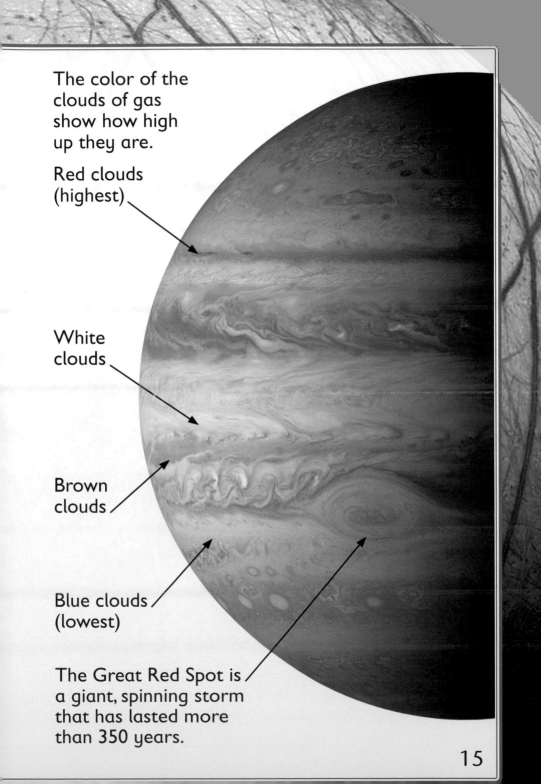

The color of the
clouds of gas
show how high
up they are.

Red clouds
(highest)

White
clouds

Brown
clouds

Blue clouds
(lowest)

The Great Red Spot is
a giant, spinning storm
that has lasted more
than 350 years.

Jupiter

Why does Jupiter bulge? What are the colorful clouds made of? How fast are the gas clouds moving? The only way for scientists to find out more about Jupiter was to send a probe to the planet.

In 1995, a probe from the spacecraft *Galileo* entered Jupiter's swirling, stormy gas clouds.

The probe detected a mix of gases in the clouds, but these were not like our clouds on Earth. Jupiter's clouds are mostly hydrogen with some helium. These are the two lightest gases in the universe. The added dash of oxygen and nitrogen gases makes mixtures that would choke us. The clouds are too dangerous for humans to breathe.

The **cloud** tops are very cold, about −234°F (−143°C). However, Jupiter is very warm inside.

The probe also picked up waves of sound coming from the planet. These made strange, eerie noises.

There was a pecking sound, which sounded like woodpeckers tapping on tree trunks. A hissing sound was like ocean waves

crashing onto a beach with
a whistling sound of whales
calling to one another.

   This creepy music was made
by the superfast solar wind from
the Sun being pushed around by
Jupiter's magnetic field. Like Earth,
Jupiter works like a giant magnet.

Over Jupiter's north and south poles, there is some amazing light action. This dancing, swirling blue glow is called an aurora. The gases above Jupiter's poles glow when the Sun's solar wind collides with them. This is another effect caused by Jupiter's magnetic field pushing the solar wind.

The magnetic field and the solar wind cannot be seen. We can only see the light effect. These auroras spread out many hundreds of miles above Jupiter's clouds.

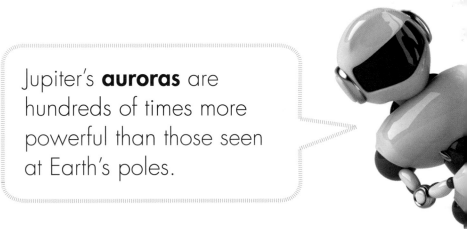

Jupiter's **auroras** are hundreds of times more powerful than those seen at Earth's poles.

Jupiter spins at a faster speed than any other planet. This makes the clouds move at very high speeds. Around Jupiter's equator (center), the clouds swirl around at more than 28,000 miles (45,000 km) per hour. This makes the equator bulge outward.

The most famous storm cloud on Jupiter is known as the Great Red Spot. This was first seen through a telescope in 1664, and has been blowing nonstop ever since.

As the probe entered the clouds, it was tossed around on a crazy swing ride as if in a hurricane. It was sucked down, too, where the temperature was much hotter. Then contact with the probe was lost. The giant planet had either crushed it, or melted it, or both.

Jupiter's Weather

It's another stormy day on Jupiter and there's no sign yet of calming down!

After six days of swirling counterclockwise, the Great Red Spot will spin clockwise once.

The air around the equator will rise and flow to the poles after being warmed by the Sun.

The cooler air will flow back from the poles to the equator.

Galileo Mission

17 ft (5.3 m) tall

Galileo was the name given to an unmanned spacecraft that was sent out to explore Jupiter and its moons. The spacecraft was named after Galileo Galilei, who used a telescope to observe Jupiter in 1610.

Galileo's timetable

October 18, 1989 Launched from the space shuttle *Atlantis*.

February 1990 Flew past Venus and propelled into a new orbit.

July 1995 Released probe. Five months later, the probe entered Jupiter's atmosphere. This was destroyed after 58 minutes in the heat and pressure.

December 1995 Reached Jupiter to orbit the planet and its moons.

1997 Main mission completed.

September 21, 2003 Dropped into Jupiter and destroyed.

Jupiter's Moons

There are more than 60 moons going around Jupiter. Four of the largest moons are Ganymede, Callisto, Io, and Europa. These four moons can be seen with just a small telescope.

Ganymede is the largest moon. It's bigger than the planet Mercury. Like many of Jupiter's moons, it is made of rock and covered in ice.

Callisto is very old and sparkles in the sky. It is Jupiter's second largest moon and the farthest one away from Jupiter. Its surface is about four billion years old and has thousands of craters.

Io is about the same size as
Earth's moon, but it looks like
a giant cheese pizza. It is covered
with the mineral sulfur, which is
usually yellow. Sulfur turns red
and then black when heated.

The black spots are active volcanoes. There are often more than ten volcanoes erupting at the same time.

The mineral **sulfur** is found in volcanic areas. It is not a metal but found as a flaky crystal. When mixed with hydrogen, its smell is like rotten eggs.

The pull from the gravity of Jupiter makes the insides of many of its moons very hot. Io is one of the hottest, which means the hot liquid rock beneath the surface is under great pressure. This liquid rock escapes to the surface as a volcanic eruption.

Pele is the name of one of Io's largest volcanoes. Its eruptions of gas and dust can rise nearly 200 miles (300 km). The ash clouds cover a huge area in a domelike shape. This is because the gravity on Io is very low.

Although the volcanoes are very hot, the surface of the moon is very cold. The thick lava flow moves slowly and cools very quickly, making strange shapes.

The top of the lava flow hardens, forming a roof of a tunnel. This keeps the rest of the lava hot for longer. The lava can flow further through the tube.

There are few **craters** on Io's surface because of the constant eruptions filling them in with lava.

Europa is about the same size as Io. It has a level surface covered in ice. There are very few craters or deep valleys. This suggests that the surface is very young and the ice is being renewed.

Parts of the surface make a crisscrossed pattern. This pattern looks like floating pieces of broken ice. This is like the ice that forms when the Arctic Ocean freezes over on Earth. Scientists think that under the icy surface of Europa is an ocean. The warmth inside the moon from the pull of Jupiter's gravity means there could be water.

Fountains of misty **water** reaching as high as the tallest mountains on Earth have been seen on Europa through telescopes.

Scientists think that there could be life in the hidden ocean. Life seems to be able to survive where water and a heat source are found. Europa may have both. Some scientists are making plans for a spacecraft to be sent to Europa to collect water samples and explore the ocean.

There are many challenges for the project. The spacecraft will need to be able to survive the trip through the asteroid belt. It will need protection from the harmful rays around the moon. It will also have to be able to land on a cracked, floating surface of ice. The sampling equipment must also not harm or pollute the ocean if it is found. Do you have any ideas for a design of a spacecraft that could travel to Europa?

Moon Zoom

These are Jupiter's four largest moons:

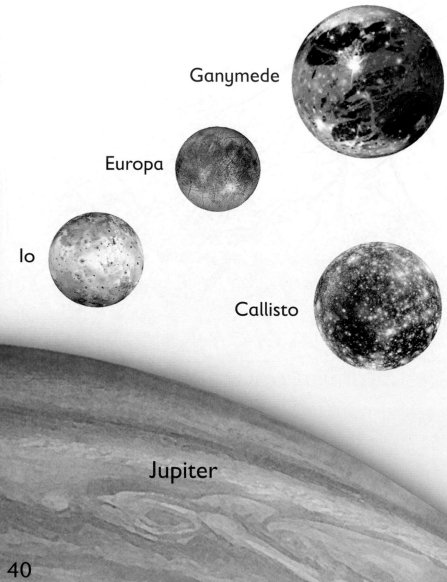

Ganymede

Europa

Io

Callisto

Jupiter

Ganymede

Rock and ice cover this large moon. Dark areas are very old craters and lighter areas show unusual grooves.

Callisto

This icy moon is said to be the most cratered object in the solar system. The glowing light areas are craters.

Io

This sulfur-covered moon is the most volcanically active object in our solar system.

Europa

This young moon has a flat icy surface that appears like broken ice floating on an ocean.

Gas Facts

Gas is a substance that has no shape. These four gases have no smell and no taste at room temperature. They are in the air around us but can't be seen.

Hydrogen is the lightest gas and the most common one in the universe. It is in water.

Helium is the second lightest gas and the second most common one in the universe.

Oxygen is the third most common gas in the universe. It is needed by most life-forms on Earth to survive.

Nitrogen makes up around 78 percent of the air we breathe. It is found in all life-forms on Earth.

Jupiter Quiz

1. Why are asteroids covered in craters?

2. What is the Great Red Spot on Jupiter?

3. How many Earth years make a year on Jupiter?

4. Why does the moon Io look like a cheese pizza?

5. What is thought to be under the ice on Europa?

Answers on page 45.

Glossary

aurora
natural light effect in the sky

crater
hollow made by an explosion or a crash

equator
invisible line around the center of a planet

gravity
force that pulls objects toward each other

laboratory
room or building used for doing scientific experiments and research

magnetic field
invisible area around a magnet where things are pulled or pushed by its force.

mass
quantity of an object

mineral
solid substance that occurs naturally

orbit
curved path around a planet or a star

probe
device that investigates unknown areas

sample
small collection of something for studying

solar wind
fast stream of gases flowing out from the Sun across the solar system

source
place where something begins

Index

asteroid 4–10, 12–13
asteroid belt 4, 7–10,
    13, 39
auroras 20–21
Callisto 28, 29, 40–41
Ceres 8, 9
clouds 11, 14–17, 21,
    22–23
    ash clouds 33
crater 5, 6, 12, 29,
    35, 36, 41
Dawn [spacecraft] 9
Europa 28, 36–38,
    40–41
Galileo (spacecraft) 16,
    26–27
Galileo Galilei 27
Ganymede 28, 29,
    40–41
gravity 6, 14, 32, 33,
    37
Great Red Spot 15,
    22, 24

helium 17, 42
hydrogen 17, 31, 42
ice 10, 29, 36–37,
    39, 41
Io 28, 30, 32–33, 35,
    36, 40–41
magnetic field 19,
    20–21
moon 12, 14, 27,
    28–30, 32, 34, 37,
    39, 40–41
nitrogen 17, 42
orbit 6, 9, 12, 14, 27
    orbital path 12
oxygen 17, 42
probe 9, 16–18, 23,
    27
sound waves 18
sulfur 30, 31, 41
Vesta 6, 9
volcanoes 31, 33, 34

Answers to the Jupiter Quiz:

1. They've crashed into each other; **2.** A giant storm that has lasted more than 350 years; **3.** 12 Earth years; **4.** Io is covered in sulfur; **5.** An ocean.

Guide for Parents

DK Readers is a four-level interactive reading adventure series for children, developing the habit of reading widely for both pleasure and information. These books have an exciting main narrative interspersed with a range of reading genres to suit your child's reading ability, as required by the Common Core State Standards. Each book is designed to develop your child's reading skills, fluency, grammar awareness, and comprehension in order to build confidence and engagement when reading.

Ready for a *Beginning to Read Alone* book

YOUR CHILD SHOULD

- be able to read many words without needing to stop and break them down into sound parts.
- read smoothly, in phrases and with expression. By this level, your child will be beginning to read silently.
- self-correct when a word or sentence doesn't sound right.

A VALUABLE AND SHARED READING EXPERIENCE

For some children, text reading, particularly nonfiction, requires much effort, but adult participation can make this both fun and easier. So here are a few tips on how to use this book with your child.

TIP 1 Check out the contents together before your child begins:

- invite your child to check the blurb, contents page, and layout of the book and comment on it.
- ask your child to make predictions about the story.
- talk about the information your child might want to find out.

TIP 2 Encourage fluent and flexible reading:

- support your child to read in fluent, expressive phrases, making full use of punctuation and thinking about the meaning.

- help your child learn to read with expression by choosing a sentence to read aloud and demonstrating how to do this.

TIP 3 Indicators that your child is reading for meaning:

- your child will be responding to the text if he/she is self-correcting and varying his/her voice.
- your child will want to talk about what he/she is reading or is eager to turn the page to find out what will happen next.

TIP 4 Chat at the end of each chapter:

- encourage your child to recall specific details after each chapter.
- let your child pick out interesting words and discuss what they mean.
- talk about what each of you found most interesting or most important.
- ask questions about the text. These help to develop comprehension skills and awareness of the language used.

A FEW ADDITIONAL TIPS

- Read to your child regularly to demonstrate fluency, phrasing, and expression; to find out or check information; and for sharing enjoyment.
- Encourage your child to reread favorite texts to increase reading confidence and fluency.
- Check that your child is reading a range of different types of material, such as poems, jokes, and following instructions.

Series consultant, **Dr. Linda Gambrell**, Distinguished Professor of Education at Clemson University, has served as President of the National Reading Conference, the College Reading Association, and the International Reading Association. She is also reading consultant for the **DK Adventures**.

Have you read these other great books from DK?

BEGINNING TO READ ALONE ②

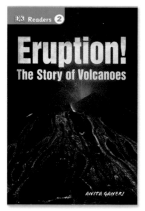

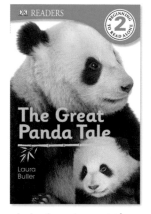

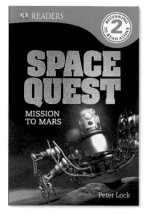

What spits out fire and ash or explodes with a bang? Volcanoes!

Join Louise at the zoo, helping to welcome a new panda baby.

Embark on a mission to explore the solar system. First stop—Mars.

READING ALONE ③

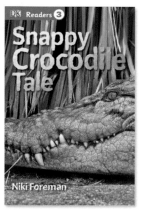

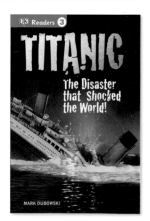

Follow Chris Croc's adventures in Australia from a baby to a mighty king of the river.

Design and test a rocket for a flying mission. Try out some experiments at home.

This is the incredible true story of the "unsinkable" ship that sank.